Minds-On
FUN FOR SPRING
Enrichment Activities for Children in Grades K-4

By Judy Beach and Kathleen Spencer

Fearon Teacher Aids
Simon & Schuster Supplementary Education Group

Editors: Sue Mogard and Marilyn Trow
Copyeditor: Kristin Eclov
Design: Rose Sheifer
Illustration: Judy Beach
Cover Design: Marek/Janci Design

ISBN 0-86653-946-8

Printed in the United States of America

1.9 8 7 6 5 4 3 2 1

Challenge a child's imagination

And you've opened up a door.

But to keep that door from closing,

You must challenge them some more!

Contents

Using Minds-On Fun for Spring

Minds-On Fun for Spring is a special seasonal supplement designed to increase a young child's vocabulary and enrich your present curriculum. The activities motivate children to stretch their imaginations and practice their newly acquired skills in creative ways!

Each month, you can challenge your class with . . .

- **A calendar** filled with suggestions for fun days that children may enjoy both at home and at school.

- **Poems** that capture the light-heartedness of the season and enrich the children's sense of rhythm and rhyme.

- **A story (or play)** that promotes creative dramatic play.

- **Questioning strategies** that encourage critical-thinking skills in the areas of knowledge, comprehension, application, analysis, synthesis, and evaluation.

- **A rebus activity** that helps children discover more about context clues in a fun way.

- **Shape booklets** that offer a creative format for journal writings, spelling practice, writing communications to parents, and other writing experiences.

- **Story headers** that motivate children to freely and imaginatively express their ideas about various topics.

- **Creative-writing activities** on seasonal topics that encourage children to use their communication skills and imaginatively express themselves.

- **A gameboard** that may be used to encourage the growth of social skills and to review and reinforce skills presented in your classroom. For example, use the blank reproducible cards to review basic math facts and have the children move tokens along the gameboard the same number of spaces as the answers. Or review vowel sounds (c__t), assigning each vowel a specific number of moves (a = 2 moves, e = 3 moves, and so on).

- **Blank reproducibles** that may be used for calendar numbers, nametags, word cards, alphabet cards, and so on.

- **Certificates** for recording positive statements that motivate and excite the children and help them grow in self-confidence.

- **Reproducible notes** that are perfect for sending short messages home to parents or for writing reward notes to the children.

- **Reproducible art** designed to jazz up memos, notes, and bulletin boards (trace onto clear transparencies and use an overhead to project the images onto a bulletin board for tracing).

MARCH ACTIVITIES

March Activities

Name _____

March

Sunday	Monday	Tuesday	Wednesday	Thursday	Friday	Saturday

Minds-On Fun for Spring © 1992 Fearon Teacher Aids

CALENDAR ACTIVITIES

Print the following activities on squares of paper the same size as the spaces on the monthly calendar. Have the children cut out the following activity cards and then paste them on different calendar days.

Did March come in like a lion or a lamb?

Get your spring clothes out.

How many words can you make from the letters in "St. Patrick's Day"?

Look in all the places where a leprechaun might have hidden his gold.

Take a nature walk. List all the green things you see.

Make up a poem about a windy day adventure.

Visit the library and read about the legend of the leprechaun.

Do some spring cleaning. Put an old sock on your hand and dust the furniture.

Did March go out like a lion or a lamb?

Spring Fever

The flowers are blooming out in the yard.
The birds are singing and it's really hard
To do my work on such a beautiful day,
When I'd rather go out in the yard to play.
I've got spring fever bad,
But it's the best fever I've ever had.
You're not sick. It's not like the flu,
When you stay in bed and take medicine, too.
To cure spring fever you don't stay in bed.
You go outside and play instead!

The Guide

At the end of the rainbow lies a pot of gold,
At least that is what I've been told.
But the end of the rainbow is hard to find.
They say a leprechaun must be your guide.
Leprechauns are not willing to take you there.
You see, it's their gold and they don't want to share.
If you catch one, however, he'll have to tell.
It's not easy. They hide so well.
So I'll keep looking and maybe some day
I'll find a leprechaun to show me the way.

Minds-On Fun for Spring © 1992 Fearon Teacher Aids

A Dragon in Flight

The wind was blowing through the trees.
It wasn't a mild or gentle breeze.
It was a wind that took your breath away
And with it all the words you'd say.

It was a day to fly my dragon kite.
It only flew when the winds were right.
I tossed it up into the air,
Knowing it would never tear.

I held onto the string so tight
I could feel the wind tugging with all its might.
It almost took me off the ground.
My brother had to hold me down.

It was a wonderful thing to see,
That dragon kite flying proud and free.
Its colors were bold, even up so high,
Gold scales glistening in a deep blue sky.

The Secret

I heard a secret just today
From the wind as it blew my way.
As it passed close by my ear,
It whispered a secret only I could hear,
"Warm days of spring are almost here!"

A Tall Tale

I was out one day flying my kite,
When out of the sky came a really strange sight.

A mean looking dragon, one hundred feet long,
Flew out of the sky and landed on the lawn.

Smoke was curling out of his nose,
And his scales were shimmering the color of gold.

His huge leather wings were deep emerald green,
And he had the biggest feet I've ever seen.

His eyes were so red they looked like a flame,
And I almost fell over when he called out my name.

I ran inside and told my mom and dad
That a dragon had landed in their flower bed.

My mom loves her flowers and boy, was she mad.
She turned to my father and just shook her head.

My father said, "Billy, you're making this up.
You've done something wrong and you're covering it up!"

I couldn't believe it. This was nothing I'd done.
The dragon is the one who had sat on Mom's mums.

Mom said, "This story's the wildest so far.
You said it was tigers when you scratched up the car.

"You always blame things on something bizarre,
Like ghosts when you broke your father's guitar.

Minds-On Fun for Spring © 1992 Fearon Teacher Aids

"It's hard to believe anything you say
When you act in such an irresponsible way."

But this time was different. I hadn't lied.
I swear there's a dragon and he's right outside.

My dad said, "Let's get to the bottom of this.
We'll look outside if you really insist!"

The evidence we found wasn't really quite clear.
It didn't quite prove that a dragon was there.

Yes, the flowers were wilted. Something a dragon had done?
Or were they just wilted from the heat of the sun?

We found suspicious claw marks on our front door mat.
Were they made by a dragon or done by our cat?

Nothing was proven. They couldn't agree
If the damage were done by a dragon or me.

There was no way to prove that my story was true,
Oh well, what else could I do?

Minds-On Fun for Spring © 1992 Fearon Teacher Aids

QUESTIONS AND ACTIVITIES FOR THE POEM

1. Who was the main character in this story?

2. What flew out of the sky?

3. Tell in your own words what happened first, second, third, and so on. Make up a new ending to the story.

4. What is the main idea of this story?

5. Have you ever made up a story when you've been in trouble? What was the strangest tale you ever told your parents or a friend?

6. Have you ever told the truth and nobody believed you? Tell about your experience.

7. Why do you think it is important to tell the truth? What happens when you don't tell the truth? List three things that might happen when you don't tell the truth.

8. Pinocchio's nose grew longer whenever he told a lie. Pretend you have some magic dust to sprinkle on people who make up stories. What would happen?

9. What did Billy learn about telling tall tales?

10. Do you think Billy's parents should have believed him? What would you have done if you had been Billy's mom or dad?

Name_____

Cut out the pictures below and paste them in the correct boxes.

I rode my ☐ down to the park to fly my ☐ before it got dark.

The wind was so strong it blew off my ☐ and blew my kite way up in a

☐ . I climbed up and got it, but skinned up my ☐ . I think it

was ☐ to call it a night!

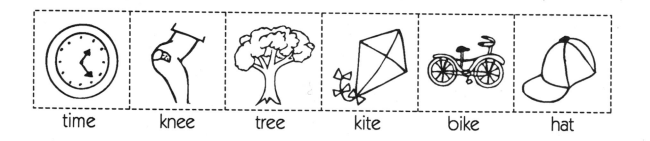

time   knee   tree   kite   bike   hat

Minds-On Fun for Spring © 1992 Fearon Teacher Aids

This booklet belongs to

_____

(name)

This booklet belongs to

_____

(name)

Minds-On Fun for Spring © 1992 Fearon Teacher Aids

Name

Name _____

A leprechaun named Shamrock O'Keefe
Opened a restaurant at the end of my street.
The name of the restaurant is the Shamrock Cafe.
It looks pretty nice in a green sort of way.
The aroma from the kitchen is hard to describe,
And the soup of the day is quite a surprise.
I have to be honest, the menu is strange,
And a few of the items I would suggest
that they change.

Make a menu for the Shamrock Cafe.

Attach to the top portion of your story.

Minds-On Fun for Spring © 1992 Fearon Teacher Aids

Attach to the bottom portion of your story.

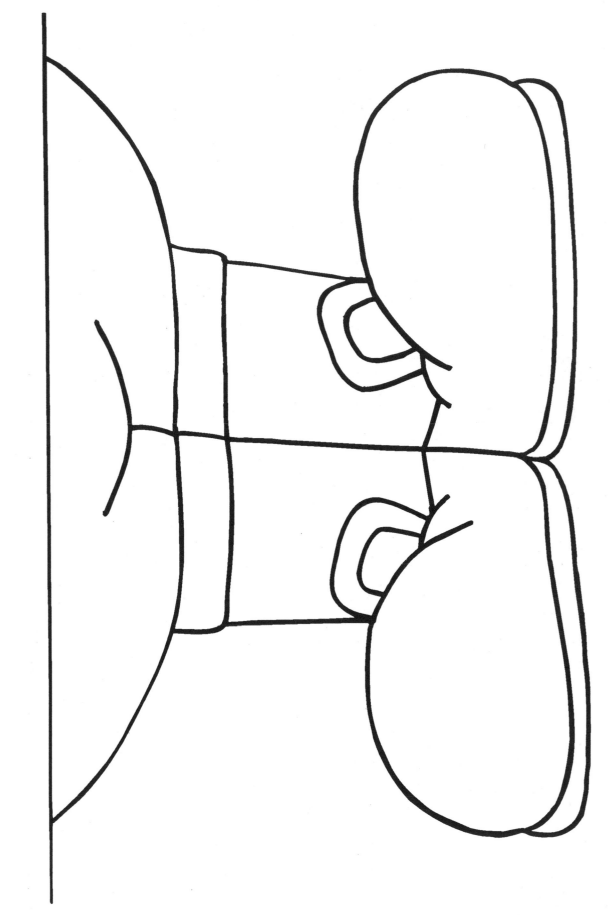

Name _____

Measles give you big, red spots.
It's almost the same with chicken pox.
With a cold you cough and sneeze.
There's always a symptom for any disease.
Except with spring fever, the symptoms don't show.
But if they did, how would you know?

Use your imagination and make up some symptoms for spring fever. Be creative!

_____

_____

_____

_____

_____

_____

_____

_____

Minds-On Fun for Spring © 1992 Fearon Teacher Aids

Name _____

The season is changing.
The air has turned warm.
The leaves on the trees
Are starting to form.

The birds are singing
From their nests in the trees.
What other signs of spring
Can you see?

You were flying your kite on a real windy day
When a gust of wind lifted you up and took you away.
When you looked down you could see your whole town.
It looked different than from down on the ground.
What would your town look like from way up in the air?
Start at your house and describe how it looks from up in the air.
Then make a map of your town as seen from the air.

Minds-On Fun for Spring © 1992 Fearon Teacher Aids

The wind blew so hard it lifted you right off the ground. Move ahead 3 spaces.

You spotted a leprechaun. Run ahead 2 spaces to catch him.

The wind blew your hat off your head. Run ahead 1 space to get it.

While being carried away on the wind, you passed over a tree. Lose a turn.

You got caught in a rain shower. Go back 3 spaces and dry off.

The tail on your kite fell off. Go back 1 space to find it.

You flew over a flag. Lose a turn.

You saw some loose balloons. Go back 1 space to catch them. Give one to a friend.

You finally came down, out of breath after your ride. Lose a turn to catch your breath.

Minds-On Fun for Spring © 1992 Fearon Teacher Aids

Name _____

Minds-On Fun for Spring © 1992 Fearon Teacher Aids

Name _____

Minds-On Fun for Spring © 1992 Fearon Teacher Aids

Name _____

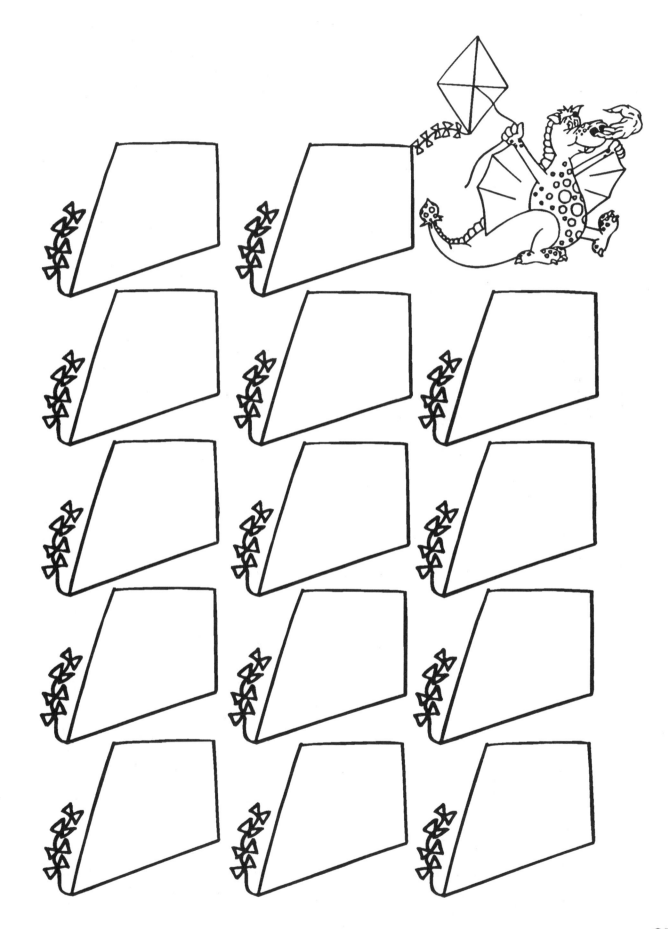

_____
(child's name)

bounced through work today!

_____
(teacher's name)

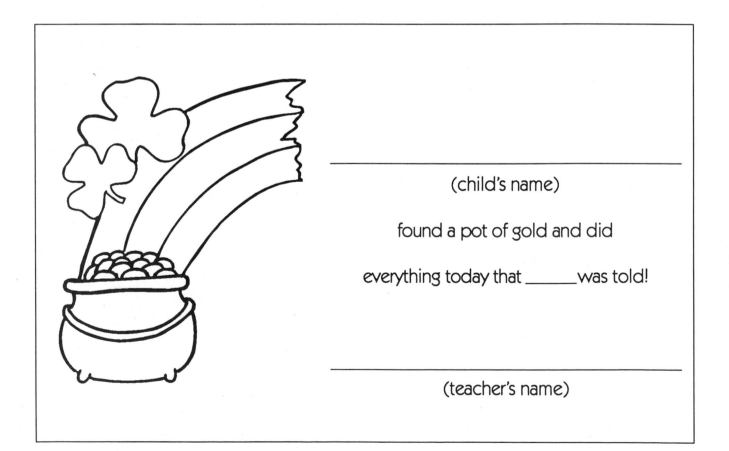

_____
(child's name)

found a pot of gold and did

everything today that _____ was told!

_____
(teacher's name)

Minds-On Fun for Spring © 1992 Fearon Teacher Aids

Minds-On Fun for Spring © 1992 Fearon Teacher Aids

APRIL ACTIVITIES

April Activities

Name _____

April

Sunday	Monday	Tuesday	Wednesday	Thursday	Friday	Saturday

CALENDAR ACTIVITIES

Print the following activities on squares of paper the same size as the spaces on the monthly calendar. Have the children cut out the following activity cards and then paste them on different calendar days.

Go for a walk. Look for some signs of spring.

Share a bag of jelly beans with a friend.

Draw a picture of yourself. Send it to your grandparents or to a special adult friend.

Color Easter eggs.

Check the weather. If it looks like rain, wear your raincoat.

Invite a friend to lunch. Make egg salad sandwiches.

Learn about Passover. Ask your librarian for information.

Send an Easter card to a secret friend.

Eat matzoh with butter and jam. Share it with a friend.

April Fools'

April Fools' is a funny day.
You have to be careful of what people say,
For what they say may not be true.
They may just be playing a joke on you.
If they are, you'll know right away
Because they'll always laugh and say,
"April Fools' on you today!"

Thunderstorm

The sky turned dark and cloudy,
And raindrops fell so hard
That soon the rain was forming
Puddles in the yard.
While thunder roared and rumbled,
And lightning lit the sky,
I watched it all so safe and warm
Inside where I was dry.

Shattered

I went on an Easter egg hunt
And I found a purple egg.
But when I went to pick it up,
I found the egg had legs.

It really looked quite funny,
Just swaying to and fro.
It didn't know just where it was,
Or where it wanted to go.

It wasn't very steady,
But still tried hard to walk.
It sort of wandered 'round and 'round
Until it hit a rock.

Of course, the eggshell shattered,
And when it fell away,
There stood a purple little chick
That looked a little dazed.

I put it in my basket
And took it home with me.
And if you don't believe me,
You'll just have to come and see!

Minds-On Fun for Spring © 1992 Fearon Teacher Aids

Teamwork

This is a story about the Easter Bunny and his friends.

Cast:
Waddles, the duck
Hannah, the hen
Chirper, the bird
Lumpy, the bear
Penelope, the skunk
Easter Bunny

Props:
Jelly beans
Easter eggs
Easter baskets
Tempera paint
Paintbrushes
Map
Sheet of paper (for a schedule)

Scene 1

Scene 1 opens a few weeks before Easter. The animals are conducting their annual meeting to review the schedule for Easter preparations. This year, as the Easter Bunny approaches the group, he overhears the others talking.

Waddles: Hannah, what's wrong? Who ruffled your feathers?

Hannah: I spend hours and hours laying hundreds of eggs, but do the children think of me? No! Only the Easter Bunny! How many eggs did he lay last year?

Waddles: But without the Easter Bunny, the baskets would never be delivered. Do you think you could do it any better?

Lumpy: Delivering the baskets is a cinch compared to getting everything packed just right, but do I get any credit? No!

Waddles: Now that you mention it . . .

Penelope: No buts about it. I slave over a hot stove making chocolate treats and jelly beans every year and do I get any credit? No!

Hannah: And what about you, Waddles? Think about it. You spend a lot of time painting those Easter eggs.

Waddles: Yeah! I spend a lot of time perfecting the design on my eggs. You're right! Who gets all the credit for our work? The Easter Bunny!

Easter Bunny: (Steps forward.) I couldn't help but overhear. I'm sorry you all feel this way, but if you think you can do my job better than I, then do it! Take the credit for it, too! I'll take a vacation this year.

Scene 2

Scene 2 opens with complete chaos in the Easter egg factory.

Waddles: Hannah, are you sure there are enough eggs? Seems like there were more eggs last year. I've got a lot of paint left over.

Hannah: The Easter Bunny always took care of that! Besides, maybe you mixed up too much paint!

Waddles: That's a possibility. Easter Bunny always measured the amount for me.

Chirper: You two had better get together because if you don't know how many eggs need to be laid, I won't know how many baskets to make.

Penelope: Well, the baskets had better be big because I've made a ton of jelly beans.

Chirper: A ton? Why so many?

Penelope: Well, I'm just the cook! Nobody told me when to stop. Easter Bunny always told me when I had enough.

Minds-On Fun for Spring © 1992 Fearon Teacher Aids

Lumpy: Should I start packing the baskets now?

Hannah: You haven't started packing the baskets yet?

Lumpy: Nobody told me to. The Easter Bunny always let me know when it was time to start packing the baskets.

Chirper: (Walks into the room holding a map and a schedule.) Have you seen this map and schedule for delivering the Easter baskets? I'm sorry, but I'm too tired to deliver them. Someone else is just going to have to do it.

All: Not me!

Waddles: I think we're all too tired to do it. We need the Easter Bunny.

Scene 3

Scene 3 opens with the Easter Bunny arriving at the factory.

Easter Bunny: I thought about what you said. Hannah, you do deserve a lot of credit for your very special eggs.

Hannah: Thank you!

Easter Bunny: Waddles, there's nobody who can decorate eggs like you do.

Waddles: Thank you!

Easter Bunny: Chirper, nobody can weave Easter baskets like you can.

Chirper: Thank you!

Minds-On Fun for Spring © 1992 Fearon Teacher Aids

Easter Bunny: As for candy, Penelope, your treats are the sweetest around. They're pure perfection!

Penelope: Thank you!

Easter Bunny: And Lumpy, what can I say? Your basket arrangements are outstanding.

Lumpy: Thanks!

Hannah: Yeah, but we found that without you, nothing gets accomplished.

Easter Bunny: Since it takes all of us to prepare for Easter, we should all get some credit. Lumpy, can you tie one of these tags on each Easter basket?

Lumpy: Sure! But what are they?

Easter Bunny: Easter tags with everyone's names on them.

Hannah: I think I speak for everyone when I say that won't be necessary. Just saying thanks was credit enough.

The scene ends with all the animals realizing the importance of each other's jobs. They go back to work organizing Easter preparations together as a team.

Minds-On Fun for Spring © 1992 Fearon Teacher Aids

QUESTIONS AND ACTIVITIES FOR THE PLAY

1. Who were the main characters?

2. What were the animals getting ready for?

3. Where did the story take place?

4. Retell the story in your own words.

5. What is the main idea of this story?

6. Why did the Easter Bunny come back to check on his friends' progress? If you were the Easter Bunny, would you have returned to help out? Why or why not?

7. Why do you think it's important for people to work together? Have you ever worked together with friends to solve a problem?

8. Do you think the animals were right to want credit for all their hard work? Was there ever a time when you wanted thanks, but never received it? Tell about it.

9. Nobody wanted to deliver the Easter baskets. How might you have solved this problem?

10. Suppose the Easter Bunny never came back. What might have happened?

Name_____

Cut out the pictures below and paste them in the correct boxes.

I went on an Easter ☐ hunt and had so much fun. I found so many

eggs, my ☐ must have weighed a ☐ . I found a green egg

next to the purring ☐ , and a yellow one inside my ☐ .

The pink one, I almost didn't see hidden high up in a ☐ . Spot, the

barking ☐ , ate ☐ or ☐ . The rest were found

by my sister, Sue.

two   basket   ton   egg

tree   one   cat   hat   dog

Minds-On Fun for Spring © 1992 Fearon Teacher Aids

This booklet belongs to

_____

(name)

This booklet belongs to

_____
(name)

Minds-On Fun for Spring © 1992 Fearon Teacher Aids

Name _____

_____

_____

_____

_____

_____

_____

_____

_____

_____

_____

_____

Name _____

The Easter Bunny had quite a few adventures on his way to deliver Easter eggs. It all started when . . . . . Tell about his adventure.

Attach to the top portion of your story.

50

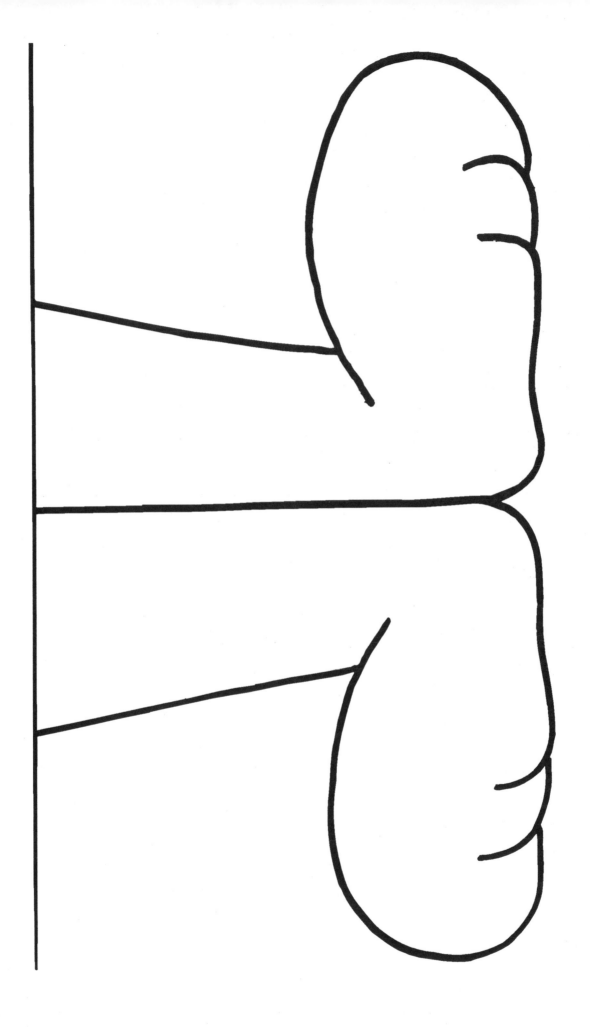

Attach to the bottom portion of your story.

Name _____

Passover is an important Jewish holiday. Learn more about this holiday.
Ask your school librarian for information about Passover. Write down
what you learn.

_____

_____

_____

_____

_____

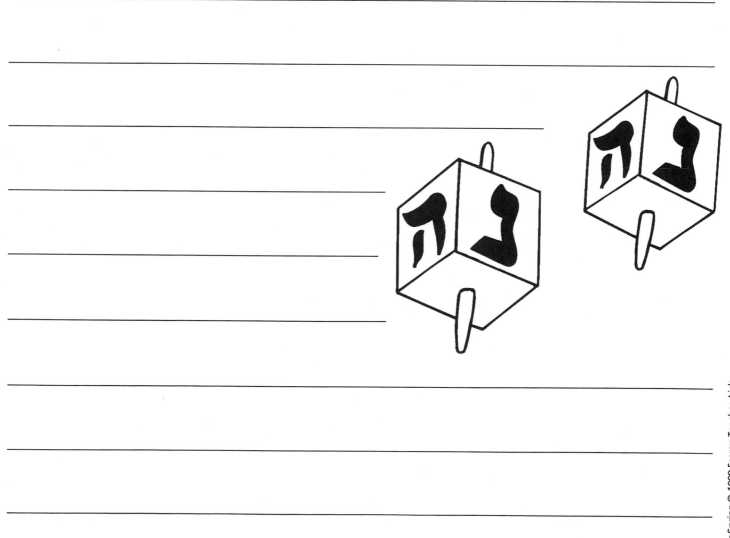

_____

_____

_____

Minds-On Fun for Spring © 1992 Fearon Teacher Aids

Name _____

Did you ever wonder what you would get
If you planted a jelly bean and kept it wet?
Maybe nothing would grow at all,
Or maybe the bean would grow into a tree very tall.
Would it have fruit or just green leaves?
Or maybe flowers that would attract the bees?
Let's pretend that it really would grow.
Just let your imagination go.

Describe your jelly bean tree. Then draw a picture of the tree.

Name _____

Raindrops falling from the sky
Look the same, but my, oh my!
When they hit things on the ground,
They all make very different sounds,
Like popcorn popping in a pan,
Or horses running on the sand.
What are the sounds that you recall
When you listen to the raindrops fall?

Use your imagination. Draw a picture in each box. Describe the sounds that raindrops make when they fall on each of the following items.

a roof	your head
an umbrella	a tin can
a window	a puddle

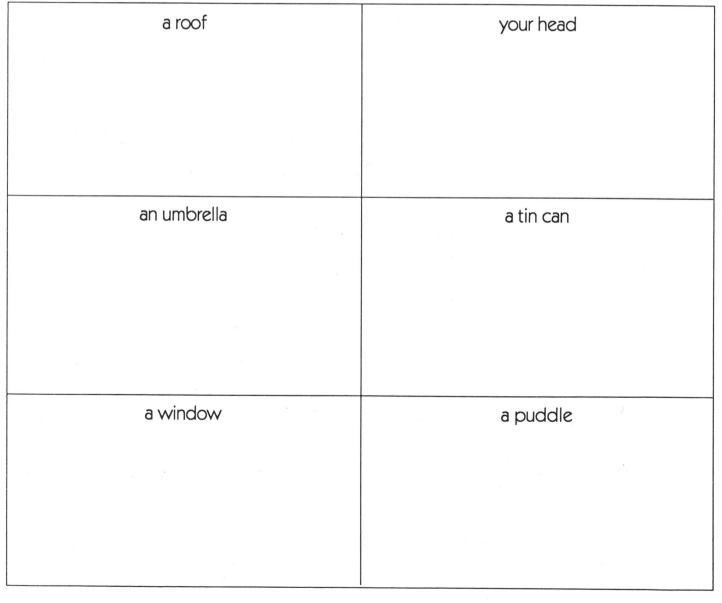

54

There's a break in the rain clouds. Run outside and play! Go ahead 3 spaces.

It started to thunder and lightning. Run home. Go back 2 spaces.

You see a big puddle ahead. Run ahead 1 space and splash in it.

You forgot your rain hat. Go back home and get it. Go back 3 spaces.

You left your wagon out in the rain. Go put it away. Go back 2 spaces.

The wind blew your umbrella out of your hands. Go ahead 1 space to get it.

Your dog got you all wet. Go home to dry off. Lose a turn.

You tracked muddy footprints into your house. Boy, was your mom mad. Clean them up—quickly. Lose a turn.

You stopped to watch a worm take a shower in the rainstorm. Lose a turn.

Minds-On Fun for Spring © 1992 Fearon Teacher Aids

Name _____

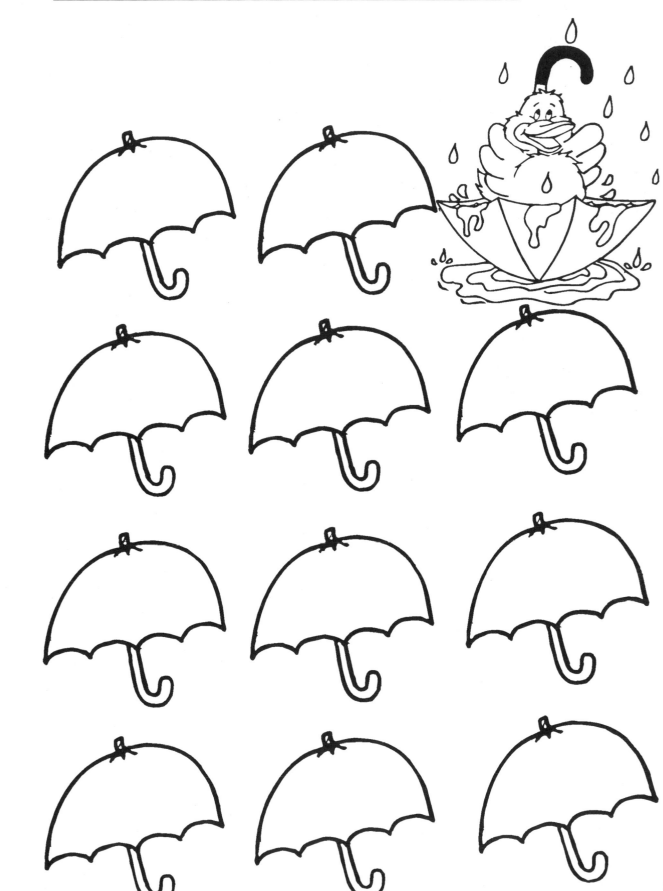

Name _____

Name _____

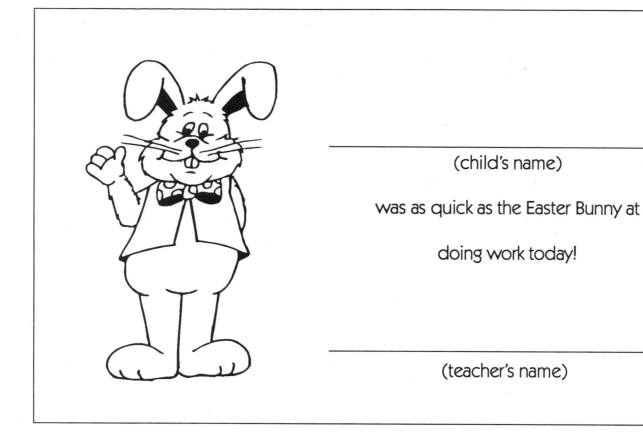

_____
(child's name)

was as quick as the Easter Bunny at

doing work today!

_____
(teacher's name)

On this rainy day

_____
(child's name)

did just "ducky!"

_____
(teacher's name)

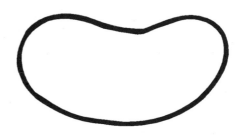

Minds-On Fun for Spring © 1992 Fearon Teacher Aids

MAY ACTIVITIES

May Activities

Name _____

May

Sunday	Monday	Tuesday	Wednesday	Thursday	Friday	Saturday

CALENDAR ACTIVITIES

Print the following activities on squares of paper the same size as the spaces on the monthly calendar. Have the children cut out the following activity cards and then paste them on different calendar days.

Go to the library. Find a book to read about whales.

Help a neighbor plant six petunias.

Start a recycling program in your home.

Water and weed your petunia plants (or other plants).

Fill an egg carton with dirt. Plant some tomato seeds.

Clean up your neighborhood. Help the environment.

Ask an adult to help you build a bird feeder. Keep track of the different birds that come to feed.

Recycle a milk carton. Use it to make a flower planter.

Set up an aquarium. Add your favorite fish.

Really Bugged

The world has many kinds of bugs,
From flying gnats to garden slugs.
They're all important, as you know,
Except one bug that has to go.

It wouldn't upset the ecology
If they were stamped out in this century.
They're rarely seen and hard to catch,
But wherever they've been, you'll find their trash.

Help stamp out Litter Bugs!

Our Liquid World

The oceans are a wondrous place
Where creatures swim with quiet grace,
Or scurry across the ocean floor,
Where humans have never been before.
We're exploring deeper every day,
Uncovering wrecks where treasures lay.
But the bounty that the oceans hold
Is much more precious than mere gold.
They give us food, but most of all,
They help to form the rain that falls.

A Tree at Last!

I'm just a seed, but watch and see,
Someday I'll grow into a tree.
Pop! Pop! Here I go!
Inch by inch I grow and grow!

My roots are spreading all around,
Searching for water deep underground.
Pop! Pop! Here I go!
Inch by inch I grow and grow!

As my branches reach up to the sun,
My leaves unfold, one by one.
Pop! Pop! Here I go!
Inch by inch I grow and grow!

All the air I breathe in,
My bark is my skin.
Pop! Pop! Here I go!
Inch by inch I grow and grow!

Now I'm strong enough to support a nest,
Or just be a place for birds to rest.
Pop! Pop! Here I go!
Inch by inch I grow and grow!

It has taken years, but as you can see,
I've grown into a big oak tree.

Minds-On Fun for Spring © 1992 Fearon Teacher Aids

Harmony

The waves were choppy and the skies were gray.
It looked like a storm was headed this way.

Out in the water you could barely make out
The head of a seal that was looking about.

Sue-Key needed shelter from the on-coming storm,
And she knew where to go to be safe and warm.

But when she arrived she couldn't go ashore.
It wasn't the same as it had been before.

There were houses and lights and the smell of humans,
And piles of garbage had washed up on the sand.

There was also a dog with large, sharp teeth
Running and barking up and down the beach.

This cove was no longer a safe place to stay.
She'd have to warn others to stay away.

Through twenty-foot waves she swam toward a bay,
While thunder and lightning turned night into day.

But in the bay where she had come for years,
Again humans were there with factories and piers.

Black, smelly clouds poured from a giant smoke stack,
Fouling the air and turning everything black.

There were chemicals in the water and oil everywhere
That got in her eyes and matted her hair.

She was struggling hard to stay afloat,
When she heard the engines of a fishing boat.

She was terrified when she felt the net,
Knowing all too well just what it meant.

She'd seen other animals besides her own
Who had gotten tangled in nets and then left to drown.

But Sue-Key was lifted up into the air
And placed on a boat with the greatest of care.

She cried out at first when the people came near,
But Sue-Key soon realized she had nothing to fear.

While they were cleaning the sludge off her fur,
She noticed other animals looking like her.

Sue-Key fell asleep feeling clean and warm.
She was finally safe from the raging storm.

QUESTIONS AND ACTIVITIES FOR THE POEM

1. Who was the main character of this story?

2. What was Sue-Key looking for?

3. What is the main idea of this story?

4. Retell the story in your own words. Then draw pictures to tell the story.

5. What signs of pollution can you find in your town? Have you ever littered? When? Where? How?

6. Why is it important to keep our world clean? What have you done to clean up your neighborhood? Make a list of ways to clean up your community.

7. Why did the people on the boat help Sue-Key? Suppose the fishing boat had never shown up. What might have happened to Sue-Key? Write a new ending to the story.

8. Why was Sue-Key afraid of the net?

9. If Sue-Key could talk, what do you think she would say about the way the world has changed?

10. If we continue to pollute, will our earth as we know it survive? What can each of us do to help clean up the earth?

Name_____

Cut out the pictures below and paste them in the correct boxes.

With my [ ] and [ ] on, I went swimming in our pond. I watched

the [ ] swimming far below. One even nibbled on my [ ] .

I found a beat-up [ ] and a broken fishing [ ] . I tried to

catch a big, green [ ] , but he swam under a big, old [ ] .

On the bottom of our pond, there's so much going on!

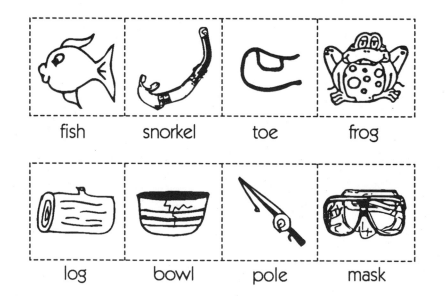

| fish | snorkel | toe | frog |

| log | bowl | pole | mask |

Minds-On Fun for Spring © 1992 Fearon Teacher Aids

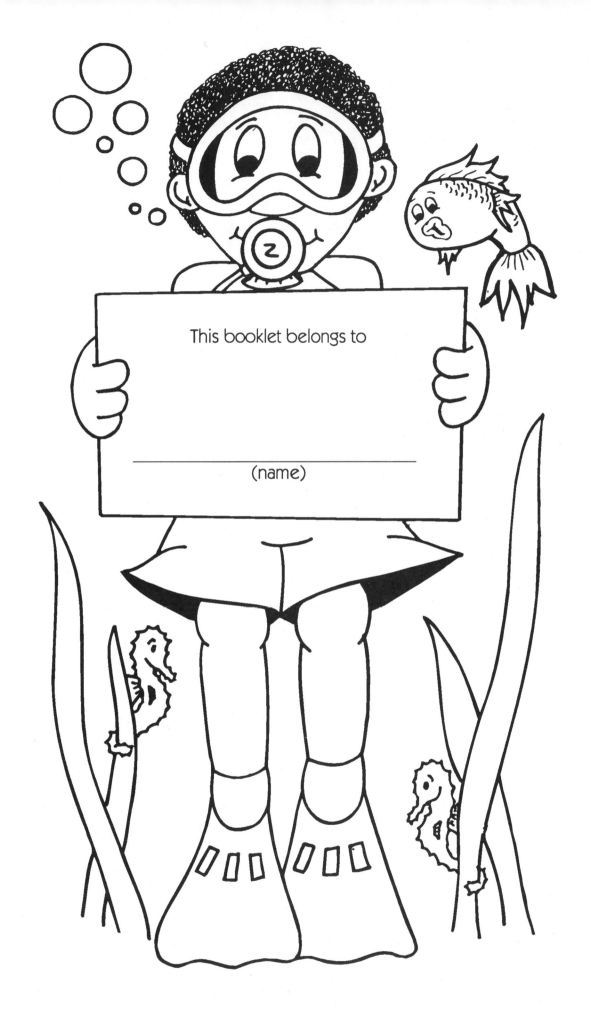

This booklet belongs to

_____

(name)

This booklet belongs to

_____

(name)

76

Name _____

_____

_____

_____

_____

_____

_____

_____

_____

_____

_____

_____

Name _____

While I was diving in the sea,
I saw an octopus watching me.
When I swam closer, I could see
That he was scared, but it wasn't of me.
He wrapped his tentacles around my legs
And pointed to a deep, dark cave.
What do you think was in the cave?

Attach to the top portion of your story.

Attach to the bottom portion of your story.

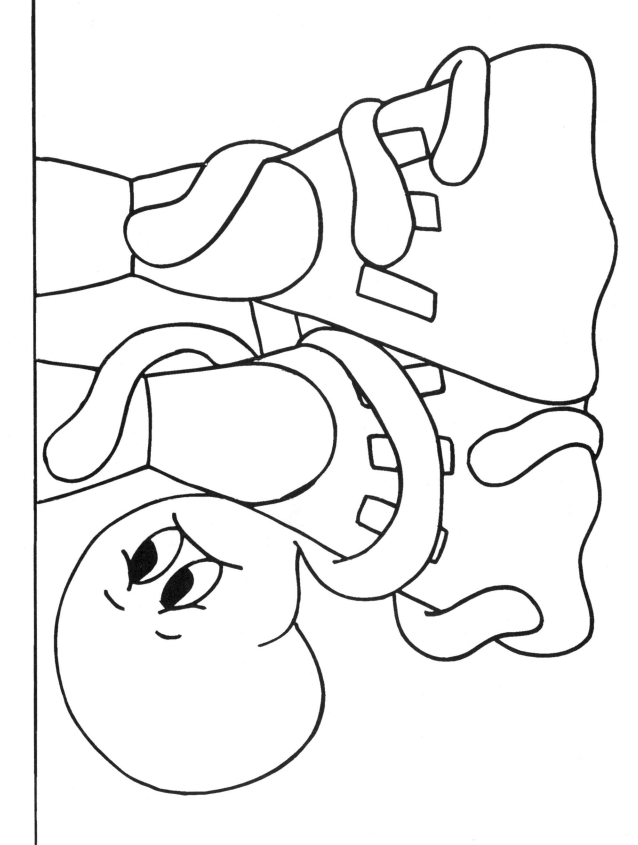

80

Name

Munch! Munch! Munch!
Wilber, the worm, was having lunch
When he was abruptly interrupted.
What happened?

Attach to the top portion of your story.

Minds-On Fun for Spring © 1992 Fearon Teacher Aids

Name _____

There's someone very special
That takes good care of me
By making sure I'm safe and warm
And get enough to eat.
She's always there to give a hug
Or wipe a tear away,
Or listen when I'm feeling sad
To what I have to say.
"I love you, Mom, so very much.
Happy Mother's Day!"

List a few of the special things your mom does just for you.
Then draw a picture of your mom.

Name _____

Be a scientist and invent
Something to clean up our environment.

Our ground is full of chemicals,
And our oceans are slick with oil spills.

There's too much pollution in our air,
And the ozone layer becomes thinner each year.

Draw a picture of your invention.
Tell us what and how it cleans.

Minds-On Fun for Spring © 1992 Fearon Teacher Aids

Name _____

A really loud noise got me out of bed.
Outside I saw a light by the shed.
It only lasted a minute or two,
But I knew right then what I had to do—
Go back to bed and wait until light.
No way was I going out there tonight!
In the morning I found this pod by the shed.
It was five inches long and glowing bright red.
It was glowing and making a weird kind of sound,
So I buried it really deep in the ground.
But a few days later, to my surprise,
Out of the ground something started to rise.

Describe what the pod looked like on Day 1.

Draw a picture of what grew
out of the ground.

_____

_____

Describe what the pod looked like on Day 5.

_____

_____

Describe what the pod looked like on Day 9.

_____

_____

With the piles of garbage that we face,
We'll soon be running out of space.
Some of the garbage will bio-degrade,
But some things won't that humans have made.

Styrofoam, plastic, aluminum, and glass
Are a few of the things that last and last.
At home there's a lot that you can do
To recycle your trash into things you can use.

A hummingbird feeder or a flower pot
Can be made from a simple Styrofoam cup.
So let your imagination go.
What can you make from the items below?

Draw a picture of each of your creations.

Plastic	Aluminum	Styrofoam

Name _____

The publishing company of "Baits and Hook"
Is putting together a seafood cookbook.
But they've run into a little snag.
They need new recipes really bad.
So think up a brand-new recipe
Using things only found in the sea.

Ingredients:

1. _____

2. _____

3. _____

Directions:

_____

_____

_____

_____

_____

_____

Minds-On Fun for Spring © 1992 Fearon Teacher Aids

You were chased by a shark! Swim ahead 3 spaces.

You had a race with a squid. Speed ahead 2 spaces.

You hitched a ride on a sea horse. Move ahead 1 space.

You swam past a buried treasure. Go back 2 spaces to claim it.

You forgot your scuba fins. Swim back 1 space to the boat and get them.

A crab hooked a free ride on your bathing suit. Go back 2 spaces to take him home.

You were zapped by an electric eel. Race ahead 2 spaces like lightning!

You were hugged by an octopus. Swim ahead 3 spaces quickly to get away.

You stopped to take a picture of a fish. Lose a turn.

Minds-On Fun for Spring © 1992 Fearon Teacher Aids

Name _____

Minds-On Fun for Spring © 1992 Fearon Teacher Aids

Name _____

Name _____

Minds-On Fun for Spring © 1992 Fearon Teacher Aids

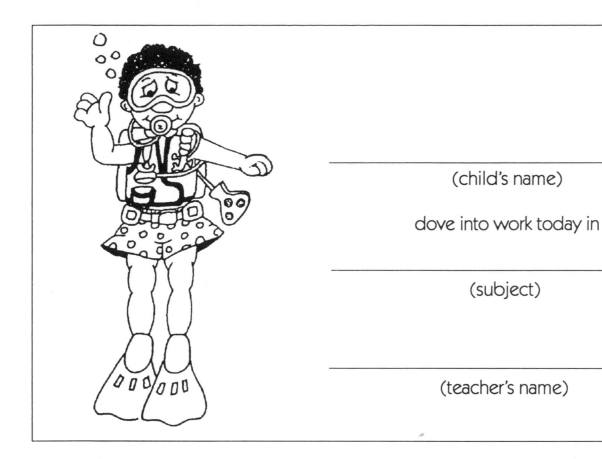

_____
(child's name)

dove into work today in

_____
(subject)

_____
(teacher's name)

_____
(child's name)

was a treasure to work with today.

_____
(teacher's name)

Minds-On Fun for Spring © 1992 Fearon Teacher Aids

Minds-On Fun for Spring © 1992 Fearon Teacher Aids

Minds-On Fun for Spring © 1992 Fearon Teacher Aids